BIODIVERSITY

ANNE O'DALY

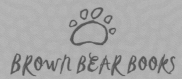

BROWN BEAR BOOKS

Published by Brown Bear Books Ltd
4877 N. Circulo Bujia
Tucson, AZ 85718
USA

and

Studio G14, Regent Studios,
1 Thane Villas, London N7 7PH, UK

© 2023 Brown Bear Books Ltd

ISBN 978-1-78121-813-6 (library bound)
ISBN 978-1-78121-819-8 (paperback)

Library of Congress Cataloging-in-Publication Data available on request

Design: squareandcircus.co.uk
Design Manager: Keith Davis
Children's Publisher: Anne O'Daly

Manufactured in the United States of America

CPSIA compliance information: Batch#AG/5652

Picture Credits
The photographs in this book are used by permission and through the courtesy of:

iStock: Izanbar 14–15, mantaphoto 12–13; Shutterstock: Mariola AnnaS 16–17, Dennis W. Donohue 18–19, Ondrej Prosicky 8–9, tarcisijo Schnaide 10–11, stockphoto-graf 6–7, Igor Trekhov 4–5.

All other artwork and photography © Brown Bear Books.

t-top, r-right, l-left, c-center, b-bottom

Brown Bear Books has made every attempt to contact the copyright holder. If you have any information about omissions please contact: licensing@brownbearbooks.co.uk

Websites
The website addresses in this book were valid at the time of going to press. However, it is possible that contents or addresses may change following publication of this book. No responsibility for any such changes can be accepted by the author or the publisher. Readers should be supervised when they access the Internet.

Words in **bold** appear in the Glossary on page 23.

CONTENTS

WHAT IS BIODIVERSITY?

Earth is an amazing place. We share our planet with millions of living things. Some are tiny, like bacteria. Others are massive, like blue whales. Biodiversity is the mixture of life on Earth.

THE WEB OF LIFE

Biodiversity is all the **species** on Earth. It is also the places where they live. Plants provide oxygen and food. Animals eat plants and other animals. All life is part of a giant network. It is sometimes called the web of life.

Number of Species

Scientists know about 1.2 million different species of animals and plants. New species are being found all the time. There may be 8.7 million species in total!

Rainforests have a high biodiversity. They cover 7 percent of Earth's surface. But they are home to more than half of all living species.

What Lives in the Amazon Rainforest?

40,000
plant species

1,300
bird species

3,000
fish species

more than 430
mammal species

2.5 million
insect species

HABITATS AND ECOSYSTEMS

Every plant or animal has its natural home. These places are called **habitats**. They provide food, water, and shelter. Some habitats are on land. Others are in water. Habitats in warm places have a high biodiversity. Those in cold places have a lower biodiversity.

ECOSYSTEMS

An **ecosystem** contains living and non-living things. It has plant and animals. But it also includes water and rocks. One ecosystem can contain many habitats. An ecosystem can be as small as a puddle. It can be as large as a coral reef. Healthy ecosystems need a balance of living things. The different parts depend on each other.

Examples of Habitats

Habitats can be on land or in the water.
Here are some examples.

Desert

Meadow

Forest

Seashore

Ocean

Coral reefs are some of the richest ecosystems. They support over a million different species. These include fish and sea turtles. One quarter of fish in the oceans depend on healthy coral reefs.

WHY IS BIODIVERSITY IMPORTANT?

Biodiversity is good for the planet. It provides food and water. Plants give out oxygen. Trees soak up **carbon dioxide**. Birds and bees carry pollen between flowers. **Microbes** keep the soil healthy.

STRONGER ECOSYSTEMS

Ecosystems need biodiversity, too. Imagine an ecosystem with just one type of plant. Small animals eat the plant. Bigger animals feed on the small animals If the plant dies out, the animals have no food. They may die out, too. Ecosystems with more biodiversity are stronger.

Animals like wolves are also consumers. They eat the rabbits.

Food Chains

Every living thing has a job. It is a producer, a consumer, or a decomposer. A food chain shows how they fit together.

Consumers can't make food. They eat it. Rabbits eat plants.

Decomposers break down dead bodies. **Nutrients** from the bodies go into the soil. Fungi and microbes are decomposers.

Producers make their own food. Green plants are producers. They need sunshine, rain, and healthy soil.

Hummingbirds drink sugary nectar from flowers. As they fly between flowers, they carry pollen. This helps the plants make seeds for new plants.

BIODIVERSITY UNDER THREAT

Biodiversity is under threat. Most threats come from people. The biggest problem is habitat loss. People clear land to build cities and roads. They cut down trees for timber. Whole habitats are destroyed.

FARMING AND FISHING

Farmers spray pesticides and fertilizers on crops. These chemicals pollute habitats. People kill animals for food. They catch fish in the oceans. Some types of fish are dying out. They are being caught faster than new fish are born.

Tropical rainforests are disappearing. People cut down 125 square miles (325 square km) every day. Most rainsforests are being cut down to make space for farmland.

Deforestation

Cutting down forests is called **deforestation**. It affects biodiversity. It causes other problems too.

Roads wear away soil.

Without trees, water runs off the land. This washes away soil. It can cause flooding.

Farm animals eat the plants.

Mud and dust from farms blocks rivers.

Soil gets blown away. This causes dust storms.

11

MEASURING BIODIVERSITY

Scientists try to protect biodiversity. They need to measure it first. One way is to count the species in an area. Counting big things is easy. It's easy to count trees in a park. It's harder to count small things, like bugs.

SAMPLES

Scientists use samples to do this. Suppose scientists want to count the number of bugs in a park. They mark out a small area. They collect all the bugs they find. They count the bugs and identify them. That helps figure out how many species there are.

Wildebeests travel to find food. They move in large groups. A herd can have thousands of animals. Scientists can't count all the wildebeest. They make an **estimate** instead.

Counting with Satellites

Whales spend most of their time in the deep oceans. It is hard to count them. Scientists use technology. **Satellites** are high above Earth. They take pictures of the oceans. The pictures are sent to a computer. Scientists look for whales in the pictures. They count them.

Counting Whales

2. A satellite's camera photographs the whale.

1. A whale swims in the ocean.

3. The image is sent to a computer.

CLIMATE CHANGE

People burn **fossil fuels** for power. This releases a gas called carbon dioxide. It traps the Sun's heat. Earth gets warmer. Our **climate** is changing.

ECOSYSTEMS

Climate change affects biodiversity. Habitats get hotter. Some plants and animals can't survive. Climate change makes weather more extreme. Floods and wildfires damage habitats. They kill plants and animals.

What Makes Climate Change

1. People burn fossil fuels in cars, homes, and factories.

2. This releases a gas called carbon dioxide. It builds up in the **atmosphere**.

3. The carbon dioxide traps heat escaping from Earth. The planet heats up.

Australia had bad wildfires in 2019 and 2020. The fires killed millions of animals.

PEOPLE AND BIODIVERSITY

People need biodiversity. Plants give us food. They provide wood, rubber, and cotton. Animals give us meat, fish, and wool.

MEDICINES

Many plants have healing powers. Ancient people used plants as medicines. Plants are still used in traditional medicine. A lot of modern drugs come from plants. A quarter of these plants grow in rainforests. By protecting biodiversity, we protect these plants, too.

Staple Crops

Staple crops are plants that people eat every day.
The main ones are maize, rice, wheat, and roots and tubers.
They provide food for about 5 billion people.

Medicines from plants are used to treat illnesses. A drug called digitalis helps people with heart problems. It comes from the leaves of foxgloves.

Maize
19.5% of the world's food

Rice
16.5% of the world's food

Wheat
15% of the world's food

Roots and Tubers
5.3% of the world's food

ENDANGERED SPECIES

Many plants and animals are **endangered**. They are at risk of dying out. Biodiversity goes down when species die out. Saving endangered species is important for biodiversity.

GONE FOREVER

If a species dies out completely, it goes **extinct**. Extinction has always happened. Human activities are making it worse. Habitat loss is a big cause. Pollution and climate change also cause extinctions. Experts think that at least 10,000 species die out each year.

Snow leopards are endangered. There may only be 4,000 left in the wild. People are trying to save them by protecting their habitats.

Sea Otters

Sea otters live in **kelp** forests. Sea urchins feed on kelp. The otters eat sea urchins. People used to hunt sea otters. The animals became endangered. Without the otters, sea urchin numbers went up. The sea urchins ate too much kelp. The sea otters were protected. Their numbers went up. The kelp grew back.

Sea otter

Sea urchin   Kelp

No sea otters

Lots of kelp is eaten

Number of sea urchins goes up

WHAT CAN WE DO?

Protecting biodiversity is important. And it's a big job. Countries pass laws to protect habitats. Some habitats have been turned into national parks. Scientists are working to save endangered species.

LOCAL ACTION

We can help, too. Protect habitats in your area. Join a local park or beach clean-up. If you have a backyard, plant flowers that attract bees. Put out water for animals. Ask your school if you can set up a wildlife area. Talk to your family and friends about why biodiversity is important.

Make a Bug Hotel

Your garden, park, or school has lots of bugs. Make a bug hotel to give them shelter. Find a shady place against a wall or fence.

Put some bricks on the ground. Lay a wooden plank across. Add more layers to make a few levels.

Make different rooms. Collect some twigs. Put them in cardboard tubes.

Use reeds or bamboo sticks for bees.

Make a nest of dry leaves, moss, and tree bark.

Add pine cones and straw.

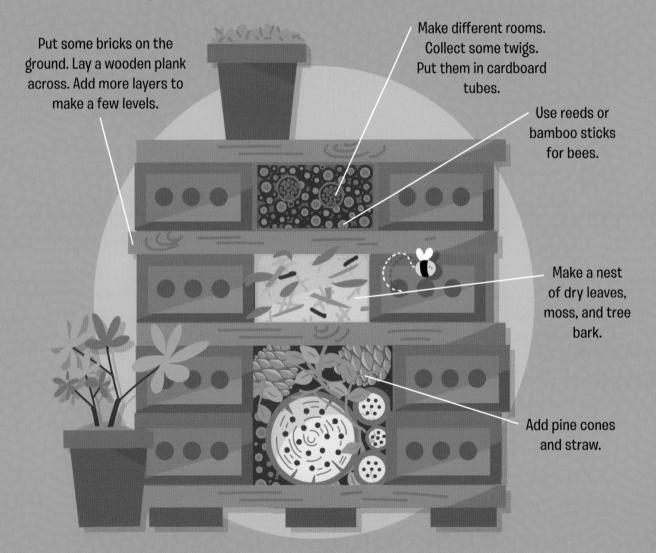

Check the hotel every few days to see what has checked in. Be careful not to disturb the animals.

QUIZ

How much have you learned about biodiversity? It's time to test your knowledge!

1. How many different species are known to live on Earth?
a. 1.2 million
b. 7 billion
c. 40,000

2. In an ecosystem, what is a consumer?
a. Someone who goes shopping a lot
b. Something that eats plants or animals
c. A plant that needs a lot of nutrients

3. What is a staple crop?
a. A crop that is only eaten at celebrations
b. A crop that is eaten every day by lots of people
c. A crop that is planted between other crops to staple them together

4. How many snow leopards are left in the wild?
a. 400
b. 4,000
c. 400,000

The answers are on page 24.

GLOSSARY

atmosphere the blanket of gases that surrounds the Earth

carbon dioxide (CO_2) a gas that humans and animals breathe out, which is also produced when fossil fuels are burned

climate the average weather in a particular place over a long period of time

deforestation clearing a forest by cutting down trees

ecosystems all the living and non-living things in an area

endangered in danger of dying out

estimate a good guess

extinct died out completely

fossil fuel a fuel that comes from the remains of prehistoric living things

habitat the place where a plant or animal lives

kelp a type of seaweed

microbes life-forms that are too small to see

nutrients substances that plants and animals need to grow and stay healthy

satellite a machine that orbits Earth

species a group of plants or animals who are similar to each other

FIND OUT MORE

Books

Biodiversity (Eco Facts). Izzi Howell, Crabtree Publishing, 2019.

Biodiversity (Map Your Planet). Rachel Minay, Franklin Watts, 2022.

It's a Wonderful World. Jess French, DK Children, 2022.

Websites

amnh.org/explore/ology/biodiversity

kids.britannica.com/kids/article/biodiversity/352854

kids.nationalgeographic.com/science/article/declincing-biodiversity

INDEX

Answers: 1. a; 2. b; 3. b; 4. b